AF441977

STATE

of

DISUNION

Text Copyright © 2020 Sandy Chapin
Photo Copyright © 2020 Sandy Chapin

ISBN: 979-8-6731492-9-4

State of Disunion

POETRY

by

Sandy Chapin

WADING RIVER BOOKS   New York, New York

Wading River Books, New York, New York 10033
© 2020 by Sandy Chapin. All rights reserved.
Printed in the United States of America

Book Designer: Joshua Chapin

Typeface: Goudy Old Style.

Cover design: Joshua Chapin

The photograph of Sandy Chapin is reproduced courtesy of Sandy Chapin and the Chapin Office.

ISBN: 979-8-6731492-9-4. FIRST PRINTING.

Queries to wadingriverpub@gmail.com

Acknowledgements.

After publishing *Entries*, in memory of the love
of my life, Harry Chapin, I began a new book
of poems about children, grandchildren, travels and
seasons: ruminations on hearth and happen-
stance. Following the 2016 election and
mornings' reading of the news, there came an
idea for a poem; a response to the stream of
disruptions in our national fabric and then
another and another and they kept on piling up.
As we have seen, one thing does lead to another.
Hopefully, we will soon be building together and
mending: to raise anew a union of justice and
respect, courtesy and concern for others and a wiser and
more thoughtful community of promise and American
perseverance.

My special gratitude to my friend, mentor and
teacher-poet, Estha Weiner, for support,
encouragement and most of all her zeal.

Table of Contents

For MARCH FOR OUR LIVES,

> the young, engaged, knowledgeable student-activists
> who have brought tremendous energy and leadership to
> the issues that threaten our integrity as a nation.

"...let America be America again. The land
that never yet has been, and yet must be."

- Langston Hughes

1. Wind

The afternoon of the wind,
I seek the sea. Too rough
to lounge on sand, I brace
myself for walking, to twist
under the gusts of lists
and chores. Clamor parts
the air, blows over plans.
I am awash in the gale
until dusk draws in a breeze;
whispers me home
to dinner and the evening news:
bluster, brazen blast,
din of this Other Wind.

2. Current Events

There is a season for oak's
appetite, for maple's juice.
In cultivated apple groves
transplants thrive. New
seeds sprout. Hardwood
and holly hold soil.

Consider the forest; that
skinny pines obstruct
light. No excuse for birch
thin-skinned shedding
or willow's bent knees, poison
ivy threading locust trunks.

Winds protest in woods;
collide. Crown of thorns
deploys. Surly
stumpage explodes,
deforests all.
Beware the kudzu.

3. How It Works

Roots, anchored to the ground,
absorb water, store energy,
germinate new cells.

Cells, in plant, convert light
to energy and manufacture
food; produce bounty.

Maple syrup, boiled down from
sweet sap, rises each spring,
produces yield for the one percent.

The tree grows larger:
all the green is at the top.

4. Cassandra

Blunt disorder disrupts tree
bark, scorches ripe grain.
Gusts clatter down every
valley; a leaf drops, the size
of a baseball glove. Slap
of the sea hits high ground.
Rises.

Winds churn fire, slash homes
to grey ash. Erosion jostles
hoards off their land. Birds
stuck in trees cancel flight.
Alien whispers; the last song.
Stars can't tell us
it's the Warming.

5. Butterfly Tree

Dune grass lifts. One monarch
glimmers towards me;
orange brindled beauty wings up,
rises higher; another and another

alight atop the sumac tree.
A canopy of butterflies
colors leaves alive and shivering.
This Fall, too warm, too late
lulls them to delay migration

three thousand miles away
to safety in the South,
in Mistec, Mexico cyamel
trees. If only I could lift
their threatened flock
to flight.

6. Curb Your Dog

Migrating birds and butterflies cease and desist.
Hazardous waste fouls sacred Indian lands.
The despot swats his scythe at parks
and canyons, axes safety shields:
Glaciers melt.

Coal plants strangle air with toxic shock.
Hydrocarbons erupt stacks of fury.
Rigs invade the wilderness.
Mountain streams froth neon slurry.

Shivering here at dawn,
even the crocus fights
to pierce the snowy crown.

7. Snow Job, 2016

Yesterday, I weeded out onion
grass around the daffodils,
their stalks erect and full-
blossomed, heads high.
Today, they bow under wet
snow as shy ladies lower
their eyes. But the news
is not about the weather.

Blizzarding thé air waves,
the candidate punishes
women again. Unbowed,
he lifts his orange mane,
thrusts his square chin,
says he has more votes
than anyone; they may carry
handguns at the convention.

These bulbs will bloom,
proving daffodils will
last longer than he does,
willing his reign
to be plowed under.

8. Alternative Facts

There's promise in the air;
this contemptuous child
has come to end despair.
Surely, you're beguiled.

He flouts abuse of power
with swaggering uncouth.
To increase his manly dower,
lies become the truth.

To elevate the Me,
Family gets the prize.
Slave of hyperbole;
smoke gets in his eyes.

Surely smoke will turn to fire;
surely flames will thrust on higher.

9. Anthem

How long will our schools be tombs?
How long will we bury our own?
How long must we cower in fear
for the next time our kids are gunned down?

No more blowing in the wind.
No more directing us to pray.
We're in this to win.
We're going to win our way.

How long will we bow to guns?
How long will we mourn alone?
How long will we vote for cowards
who get paid to sustain our ruin?

10. Halloween Parade, 2017

Slurping in the swampland's slush,
Grand Marshalls of the goon's brigade,
platoons beneath a great white moon:
"Hail to Halloween Masquerade."

Brash Breitbart megaphone,
Witch, riding Alt-right's bogus broom,
to brush out order, sweep in chaos:
White Supremacist's eager groom.

Turtles burrowed in Party shells;
two Ghosts of Congress past,
stripped of authority's balls,
emasculate puppets now unmasked.

Stooge of Russian oligarchs,
Citizen Cyprus launders plunder,
captures White House fealty:
Monster splays all rules asunder.

Ghoul would throw gays in the clink;
enemy of women's options
pins a plaque of Ten Commandments
on the Chamber's Constitution.

Mad movie megalomaniac,
power wielder, briber, stalker,
gropes and rapes young starlet beauties;
Devil's secret buyoff shocker.

Global Warming's chief denier,
appropriates a British title;
bankrupt Bat of greed and fraud,
shrieks out tweets to feel vital.

Pinnacle of the leader's rage,
blasts venom upon Justice's probe.
The angry crook collects our bounty
to sabotage a hopeful globe.

11. Progress

Childhood's GPS was a trip:
neighborhood, walk to school,
eight-mile bike to a cliff over
the Charles. *Explore! it said.*
Bird calls. Fall leaf burns.

Indoors, the radio conjures
The Shadow, voices painting
pictures on the story road.
TV tied the strands of sight
and sound: no taste, no touch,
no scent. From print to cursive
to type. Fingers on the trail,
send and receive the U.S. Mail.
Laptop next, search and find,
type and send, scroll and buy.
Now, iPhone commands
a universe. No need for feet.
One finger pulls from the deep
black hole, this virtual world
in my hand, stripped of honey.

12. History Lessons, 2018

In 1903, two bicycle makers
from Ohio defied gravity
with the first 12-horsepower
airplane engine: Flight.
At Fort McHenry in 1812,
our army, under rocket's red
glare, manned the air
and took over the airport.

President Andrew Jackson,
a Tennessean slave owner,
died in 1845.
He was really angry with regard
to the Civil War and never
would have let it happen.

Have you heard of Harriet Tubman?
She was very, very courageous.
Believe me. She should
be placed on the $2 bill.

13. Truth and Consequences

Much of the sensibility and hardness of the world
is due to the lack of imagination which prevents a realization
of the experiences of other people.

Why should we accept
           immigrants from shithole countries?

Fear of the opinion of others and hesitation
to tell the truth that is in us in the divine floods
of light, no longer flows with our souls.

FAKE NEWS media knowingly doesn't tell the truth
           —a great danger to our country,

People who shut their eyes to reality
invite their own destruction.

Climate change — a hoax, fictional, mythical,
           a con job, bullshit, laughable.

The battle we have fought and are still fighting
for the forests is part of the eternal conflict between right
and wrong...so we must continue striving for those trees.

We must withdraw conservation policies that burden
the development of fossil fuel production.

What's wrong with our children? Adults telling
children to be honest while lying and cheating.

America has the cleanest air in the world.
We don't make windmills in the U.S.

A very stable genius!

The best way to get the sons of bitches
*   is to laugh at them.*

NOTE: *First Stanza:* Jane Adams
Third Stanza: Elizabeth Cady Stanton
Fifth Stanza: James Baldwin
Seventh Stanza: John Muir
Ninth Stanza: Marion Wright Edelman
Final Stanza: Molly Ivins

14. Independence Day

We spark the night sky,
celebrate America's Birthday:
liberty and justice for all
at the Statue of Liberty.

Fathoms away on the National Mall,
Self-Appointed Favorite President
sets up a campaign rally
at the Lincoln Memorial, marches
military might, power, prestige;
bloviates undaunted superiority,

confines migrant children in detention
camps, separates nursing
infants from their mothers, leaves
children to die from untreated infections.

North, at the entrance to New York Harbor
and Ellis Island, we hail the Lady's flame:
Send these, the tempest-tossed to me.
I lift my lamp beside the golden door.

15. Present from France

Her statuesque simplicity
holds honored customs in her crown.
However the world may change,
her torch flames forth the light,
a pledge, a hope enduring:
the purpose of the gift.

16. Human Flow

Inspired by the film by Ai Wei Wei

A drone zooms in on ten thousand wriggling ants
        invading foreign fields.
Their bodies scurry, carry clothes,
        sacks and young toward barbed wire.

The bulging rubber raft furrows forward, tossing wake;
        bundled things cling
and sink. Helicopters hover. Small boats and waders
        sling ropes, pull the load ashore.

Shanty hovels rent asunder. Wind shreds tarps,
        cuts clotheslines, topples wrecked tents,
sweeps sandstorms over stumbling hoards
        bent under bales. Again the flotsam moves.

Children play.

17. Immigrants

Please, no strangers, here
in the desert sandhills
of junipers and cottonwoods.
Hohokam brought corn;
Puebloans followed deer,
hunted, gathered

and planted canyonlands.

Athabaskan tribes crossed
the Bering Straits, drove
South. Navaho farmers
and sheep herders moved

into cliffs in ancient sites.

Juan de Oñate led
Conquistadores to seize
the Seven Golden Cities
of Cibola, to build camps

on forced Indian labor.

Taos Indian, Pope, spurred
rebelion with his knotted-
rope calendar; kicked out
the Spanish to El Paso.

Kept them out for a dozen years.

From the South on Camino Real,
the Santa Fe Trail, East
to West; traders, outlaws,
miners, loggers, soldiers

mobbed the New Mexico Territory.

The United States Army
installed governors,
bribed and conquered.
Arizona and New Mexico

were annexed to the Forty- Six.

Now, Mexican children of Spanish
conquerors and their Indian
slaves, cross the border
of junipers and cottonwoods
in the desert sandhills.

Please, no strangers, here.

18. From Syria

North over 2,300
miles, above
the Arctic Circle,
pelted by hailstones
and icy winds,
huddled in summer
clothes, they
stagger on bikes
across the border
to Storskog.
Each backpack
is a lifeline;
jacket, liter
of water, coins.

Left behind is living:
job, school, market,
hearth, books,
photos, neighbors,
friends. Displaced
now, a new story
spits out of muscle
and mind; no rest
and never again
home.

19. Sh*thole Countries

*Why are we having all these people from shithole countries
come here?" asked the President of the United States.*

Everyone knows Frida Kahlo, the eyebrows, iron will
Self-portraits with exotic birds and monkeys,
Wearing huipiles and rebozos to champion
Mexico's indigenous people. She made Mexico famous.

Fela created Afrobeat: American funk and jazz,
mixed with traditional Yoruba music, broadcast
around the world to protest corruption
until the Nigerian government sent
one thousand soldilers to end his performances.

Columbian, Gabriel Garcia Marquez' stories of magic
realism fertilized world-wide interest in Latin
American literature through nine generations
Of his country's conflict and regeneration.

The world watched while Nelson Mandela
was arrested and imprisoned for 27 years for railing
against apartheid in his native South Africa.
Finally, protests, boycotts and sanctions freed him
and he was elected President.

From Earth's fertile soil
arise creatures great and small.

20. Circus Maximus

There's a new circus in town!
Visit the row of cages:
of detained, trapped "animals;"
constrained by customs agents.

Next, the Freak Show;
line-up of insiders' cells;
showoffs, contortionists,
dwarfs lobby for spoils.

Ready for the Three Rings?
Running up and down,
jockeying for position,
the hungry crowd of clowns.

The Second ring of trapeze acts,
jugglers, acrobatic stunts,
flout all safety rules,
as serious peril mounts.

Ring Three, the lion tamer;
appointed to temper the roar.
He bravely enters the room,
quickly gets shown the door.

Watch now! The Ringmaster,
the new P. T. Barnum, calling the shots,
raises his baton, rouses the crowd,
the hawker, with everything he's got.

So, hail to the Romans
who taught us the game:
Bread and Circuses pacify,
divert attention. Above all, entertain!

21. Saturnalia

Jesus was born in Bethlehem
in Springtime. Remember how lambs
on the hillside lay. The first
Christians concealed themselves
in the processions of celebrants
of the Feast of Saturnalia,
carrying boughs of greens,
holding candles, starting bonfires
to preserve the light from passing
into eternal darkness.

This season's descendent of Herod
the King, gathers his paltry priests
to boost his power, presents unto himself
gold and myrrh and frankincense
as he casts out the child.

During this diminution of the light,
we await Spring lambs.

22.   The Christmas Nativity

He sets up the stable
and the empty manger,
positions all the figures,

pulls out the Jews,
pulls out the Arabs,
pulls out the Foreigner.

All that is left is

one jackass

and a bunch of sheep.

23. Sacrilege

I am the king of Israel
and the Second Coming of God.
I frolic in green pastures,
receive each day my daily bread.
My cup runneth over;
I shall not want.
I will fear no evil; my rod
and my staff shall comfort me.
My Will be done.
I dwell in the House
as the Chosen One,
Forever.

24. A Christmas Story

And it came to pass in those days,
that there went out a decree
from Caesar Augustus that all the world
should be taxed. And Joseph went up
from Galilee, out of the city of Nazareth
into Judea, unto the city of David,
which is called Bethlehem, to be taxed
with Mary, his espoused wife,
being great with child. And so it was
that she should be delivered.
She brought forth her firstborn son
and laid him in a manger, because
there was no room for them at the inn.

And now, families go forth to apply
for asylum where there is no shelter,
where infants are separated
and sequestered in squalid camps.

Behold there came wise men from
the East to Jerusalem, saying,
Where is he that is born King
of the Jews? For we have seen
his star in the East, and are come
to worship him. Lo, the star
went before them and stood over
where the young child was
with Mary his mother. They fell
down and worshipped him
and presented unto him gifts.

Rohingya flee from the East
from violence and genocide, They
leave all gifts behind and huddle on
their knees in military encampments,

And when the wise men were departed,
behold, the angel of the Lord appeareth
to Joseph in a dream, saying, Arise,
and take the young child and his
mother, and flee into Egypt, and be thou
there, until I bring thee word, for Herod
will seek the young child to destroy him.

From bombs and bullets, families flee
for Egypt and Jordan, struggle
in poverty, scattered into crowded
tent cities without medicine or food.

Infants are born daily on cold floors.
There is no room at the inn.

25. Morning in the House

Choose the news,
lay out clothes
arrange hair, practice scowls
in the mirror. Who knows

what the enemy is planning?
Apply tan and fresh cologne,
a red tie. No need
for meetings. You're known

for intuition when it comes
to foreign and domestic matters.
His interim appointments
invite anyone who flatters.

Leave the grooming, dressing
table, shower and sink,
tweet on the toilet but
remember not to drink.

26. Humpty Dumpty

Humpty Dumpty's incredible gall
promised his base a beautiful wall.
All the king's horses
and all the king's men
couldn't undo the message he sent.

Humpty Dumpty called up the Guard
to save us from rapists and murderous hoards.
All the king's swindles
and all the king's lies
fattened his image in too many eyes.

27. Legacy

George Washington crossed the Delaware,
routed the British, convened Congress
to pronounce the peoples' independence.

Abraham Lincoln debated his way
to the presidency, promoted abolition,
emancipated slaves, restored the Union.

Franklin Roosevelt led us out
of the Great Depression, invented jobs,
forged victory over the Axis.

Barack Obama passed the Affordable Care Act,
made the Iran Nuclear Deal, engineered
the Trans-Pacific Partnership Agreement,
to temper China's trade dominance,
for cooperative regional exchanges.

His successor ordered tariffs on China,
which forced China to cut soybean imports,
which hurt U.S. agricultural economy,
which led to subsidies for farmers,
which are paid for by tax payer dollars,
which led Brazil to burn rain forests,
which clears land to grow soybeans,
which feeds pigs, for exports to China,
to answer China's demand for pork.

28. Monkey: Vide Audi Tace

In 1392, French balladeer, Eustache Deschamps,
wrote: to live in peace, one must have
the eyes of a mole,
the ears of a herring,
the mouth of an elephant.

From the 17th century, three monkeys
in the Buddhist proverb
I do not see,
I do not hear,
I do not speak,
travelled from Japan
into the creed of the Mafia.

Today, we have one monkey, merchant
of monkey shines, Peck's Bad Boy
of deadly monkey business.

29. Revolution

Not swayed by the news,
nor despondent, though the rants
hammer the head. Frequently,
History repeats itself.

The Roman Empire builds, invents,
masters, flourishes. Then for four
hundred years, sits, fat, consumes
the products of her invention.

Timbuktu, medieval center of trading
salt and gold, seat of Islamic
culture, capital of scholarship:
an empire that erased itself.

Don't ever believe man
conquers nature. Grains
sift through the hourglass
and pollinate: call and response.

The moon presents a new phase
every night; always veering
toward revision or renewal.
On her face, find inspiration.

30. Words Wield

A whisper festers in the air;
Wuhan, at the other side of the world.
Do you remember when they said
you could dig a hole in your yard
and eventually reach China?
Scattered scraps of voices
veer against the wind.
Virus. Spread.
We, knowing how to wait out words, wait.
Contagion. Risk. Tests.
Wheeling transit navigates the globe.
Shutdown. Detain. Close.
The word engine churns.
It knows how to grow
land chopped into pockets.
Threat. Containment. Severe.
Relentless relearning of what we know.
Joblessness. Isolation. Lockdown.
New raging words proliferate.
Ventilators. ICU. Death.
Silence.

31. Roots

This is about remote learning,
of lessons never taught before.
After the student's eight-hour night
shift, he can't wake up anymore.

They pack bags, summon the driver
and staff, lock up the city doors,
painted with fear, race to segregate
their prerogative at the shore.

After three-hours sleep, grabbed scrubs,
N95, gloved for dread, left child alone to home
school, caught the subway to Elmhurst,
another double shift in the death zone.

Homebound teacher, two preschoolers,
medical worker husband; no letup:
cooking, shopping, washing, stranded.
Terror to bear in the dark; close–up.

Their entrenched health, intertwined,
rooted in disease, capable of devastation.
We are all in this together.

Some of us much more than others.

32. Outbreak

Clumps of daffodil leaves press
through mulch by the mailbox.
A touch of pink on the Redbud tree.

Early warning slips slowly from New York;
one hundred spread from a single man.
A square-mile containment town for testing.

The sunny side of Andromeda blooms.
Cascades of lime-green willow fronds
swing and play across the park.

The rampant scourge has swept
across all lands and oceans,
spreading panic, begging caution.

Crocuses and Glory-of-the-Snow lift
through pachysandra, edging beds.
Daffodil buds rise and flower.

Denial fuels the crisis' fury.
Too late, the cry for masks and beds.
Virus ravages across the map.

Overnight the forsythia bursts gold.
A clarion call, boisterous, brazen brights
every yard and hillside, fence and wall.
Abundant. Cultivation: the gods align.

33. Gardening

You, alone, are up.
You plot: pull
grasses from
the gravel driveway,
crabgrass from
the patio grout.
root out dandelion
faces' rude affront
in cultivated beds.

Look beyond weeds:
ahead, there is fertile soil,
patient for use. Plant a seed,
root slowly to leaf,
day's warmth
underneath. The deed
of your hands might sprout
something new. The seed
might wrestle through.

34. Green

Greenbacks for grabs, embezzled, sneak offshore
to Swiss vaults. His dirty deeds
up for ransom, illuminate once more
thin distance between green and greed.

Is he a gullible hack, an unstable knave,
moving expeditiously, duped by some aide
or does his experienced deceit crave
stashed stuff in self-anointed accolade?

So, the emerald sea to shining sea:
his America, flush on seething plain.
Blind to the verdant majesty;
the grassy grace of God's domain.

Green is the virgin bud fresh from snow,
the neon worm the robin pulls away
from wetted lawn; green, the smell that sows
the soil, pulling promise into prayer.

35. Gaia Healing

Eagles return to the Hudson.
Wolves multiply at Yellowstone. We
breathe the cleanest air in a dozen years.
Coyotes, pumas, javelinas stroll urban streets.
Sea turtles nest on beaches, undisturbed.
Indians suddenly see
the Himalayas one hundred miles away.
Gaia exhales in the deep.

She rises overland, procreates: sky
sea, mountain but the last of her
progeny, Chronus, swings the scythe:
forest fires, hurricanes, earthquakes,
rising oceans, pathogens, to renounce
the gifts of Gaia. God of time,
destructive force, destructive foil.

This war has enemies within,
Earth wails. Bring Chronus down.
Arise Gaia.

36. Behold

We trudge each land bridge span
Southward to brave strange lands.
In steerage, we risk hostile seas; outrace
the past; new presents to embrace.
We plunder forests, blinder graves,
all legacies of natives and our slaves.
Restless pioneers tramp West, seed new
frontiers, scale Rockies to Pacific views.
Steamboats speed, factories abound,
breed untried things, break new ground.
Trains carry cargo, freight, war stuff
across the plains; never quite enough.
Highways forge new trails, expand
jazz and blues and jails and contraband.
Our wheel of voices scores the loudest song.
Today entreats, *what have we lost along
the way?* To construct the towers, concrete the quag,
newcomers fill the nation's flag,
conquer fields, mountains, skies,
remake it all to seize the prize,
unwrapping leaves of infinite intention
to smite the old, fast forward fresh invention.

America will sink and swim, yet one small word,
aspire, may propel our fragile union forward.

About the Author.

Sandy Chapin is the author of the book of poems, *Entries*, and writer of lyrics for *Cat's in the Cradle*, which entered the Grammy Song Hall of Fame in 2010. She also wrote the lyrics for the film score of the television movie, *Mothers and Daughters: The Loving War*, and the lyrics for *Diary of Lights* by Adrienne Kennedy. She lives in New York City.